D0912648

The Nun Factory and Other Horror Stories

by

Barbara Junod

authorHOUSE™

1663 LIBERTY DRIVE, SUITE 200
BLOOMINGTON, INDIANA 47403
(800) 839-8640
WWW.AUTHORHOUSE.COM

First published by AuthorHouse 10/08/04

ISBN: 1-4184-9717-7 (sc)

Printed in the United States of America
Bloomington, Indiana

This book is printed on acid-free paper.

I dedicate this book to my family: mom and dad, grandparents, aunts, uncles and cousins who are gone – to my sisters, aunts, uncles and cousins that are still here. I miss you still.

Table of Contents

Chapter 1
The Nun Factory

My mother had often accused me of reading a book during her most emotion-packed moments. According to mom, I've done this since birth. Can you imagine the doctor saying, "Look, it's a girl and she's reading 'Lassie, Come Home'." Observing an experience like that would certainly stop the people who brag that their two-year old is already reading light novels.

The truth, though, is that I was not reading "Lassie, Come Home" when I was born. I didn't read that fine classic until I was in the seventh grade. I know this for a fact because, being a compulsive list maker, I've kept a list of every book I've ever read and when I've read it. You've heard of "The Book of Lists"? Well, this is the list of books.

This list of books has its advantages. For instance, if I want to find out what I was reading at O'Hare Airport while I was waiting to accompany my mother on her first airplane trip, certainly an emotion-packed moment for her, all I have to do is look at the list and see that I was reading "Centennial", and, considering its size, I probably was reading it for a good long time after that trip. In fact, I had probably not gotten past the dinosaur era three months later.

By referring to my trusty list I can tell you that on a day in June, 1958, I was in the back seat of the family car trying to finish "Wuthering Heights". I had to finish it quickly so that mom could return it to the library when mom, dad, and my sisters went back home. I would not be going back with them because I was entering the convent – another emotion-packed moment in mom's life.

I have since heard of various last minute, symbolic things that girls have done before entering the convent, like crushing out their last cigarette on a pillar of the Motherhouse gate. But my finishing "Wuthering Heights" had nothing to do with symbolism. I just wanted to finish the darn thing so that I could list it.

If my memory serves me correctly, (and I have every right to think that it won't, as this has been thirty years in the writing), I finished the book just about the time that we pulled into a gas station in the city of our destination. It was at this gas station that I would miraculously change from a tomboy, wearing jeans and a checked blouse, to a young lady seeking admittance into a religious congregation. Amazing what a change from jeans to a skirt can't do.

As I entered the women's room, my mother tearfully grabbed the book out of my hand and replaced it with a wad of Kleenex. The last gas station restroom in America to have toilet paper was a Sunoco Station in Peoria, Illinois. A little, old lady had brought her own and had forgotten to take it with her when she left. She was on her way to the World's Fair of 1934.

The change of clothes was made and we traveled the rest of the way to the Motherhouse. If you never have seen the grounds of a Motherhouse, it is a city unto itself. This particular one had a grade school/high school building and a college for girls, plus the dormitory buildings for the boarders of the two schools and the nuns who staffed them. Then there was the Motherhouse building itself. It housed the high potentates of The Order, and, up on the third floor, the postulants.

I was about to become a postulant. If I made it through six months, I would move to the Novitiate. After a year as a novice, I would take my first vows and be sent to one of the many schools either owned, or at least operated by The Order. After sixty or seventy years of teaching, my mental health would probably give out and I would be brought back to the Motherhouse to work in the Laundry and/or die in the Infirmary. I would then be buried in the Motherhouse cemetery. This would be my life. I could hardly wait to get started on such an exciting and promising future for I was young and filled with religious fervor.

We had no sooner arrived at the Motherhouse on that bright summer Sunday in June when my sponsor found us and whisked me away to help me put on my postulant outfit.

A sponsor was the nun who had gotten you interested in the whole thing in the first place. This Sister had taught me in high school and I had the kind of crush on her that was common to many Catholic girls toward the nuns that taught them. My mother often thought of suing this nun for alienation of affections. Mom didn't want me to enter the convent, but she was afraid she'd go to hell if she stood in my way. My father wasn't Catholic, so thought the whole thing stupid in the extreme.

My sponsor, who looked like a female version of Bishop Fulton J. Sheen, in full nun's headdress and long habit, introduced me to a friend of hers that first afternoon.

"Dear, if you ever need anything, go to Sister_
_____"

(Name withheld to protect the guilty.)

Flippantly, I said, "I'll look you up sometime, Sister".

She gave me a strange look, which meant nothing to me at the time, but it just so happened that this nun turned out to be the Postulant Mistress. Yes, Virginia, that's what they called her. It would have made more sense to call her a Madam, what with her being in charge of a house of about one hundred young women, but it was Mistress, and she was to be my boss for the next six months. I did not make a good first impression.

There were about seventy-five who had entered with me and also a group of postulants who had joined the previous February. One of these February postulants was assigned to each of us. Their job was to show us the ropes and help us and so they were called our guardian angels. My guardian angel was a girl from my high school back home. She had entered when she was a junior in high school, so she was chronologically younger than I, but older "in religion". Because she had entered before I had, she considered herself quite superior to me and was fond of saying things such as,

"When I saw you in high school, I thought you were pretty dumb, but I guess you're smarter that you look." – a left-handed compliment if I've ever heard one.

We sat on the lawn that afternoon, my parents, my sponsor, my guardian angel and myself, along with seventy-four other groups of parents, sponsors, guardian angels and new postulants. What with trying to adjust to my new garb of long black skirt, blouse with white cuffs and collar, black cape and veil, black stockings and granny-type shoes, I heard none of the conversation. I have no idea what I said to my parents and my sisters before I was to leave them forever, or, at least until the first time they could visit, three months later. A bell rang, the first of many, and the next thing I knew, my sponsor and guardian angel were taking me up the steps into the entrance hall and down the highly polished, long, narrow hall leading to the huge Motherhouse chapel.

The double doors opened to row upon row of pews. Stalls on both sides of these pews faced the middle aisle. The postulants occupied the pews toward the front. The junior professed and professed sisters' places were the rest of the pews in the back of the novices and postulants; they were also in the stalls on both sides. The professed sisters were those who had already taken their final vows. The junior professed had taken vows for one year and would renew these vows every year for the next five years if they chose to stay in The Order.

My guardian angel took me to one of the front pews. I knelt down, but she said,

"You better sit. When we start praying, you're not going to believe what happens."

She was right. They began to chant the "Office of the Blessed Virgin", in Latin, of course, this being pre-Vatican II. This, in itself, wasn't too strange, but the chanting alternated from one side of the chapel to the other, and while one side sat, the other side stood facing them, and then, at the Gloria Patri, at the end of each section, both sides stood and bowed toward each other. Then the other side sat. I could see why they wanted the new postulants to sit this first one out. It would be a long time before we would get the choreography down pat.

After what seemed like a long time of ups and downs, we filed out of the chapel in silence and went downstairs to the postulants' refectory – nun talk for dining room. There were signs welcoming us. I expected a big meal to also welcome us – probably steak, potato and sour cream, nice tossed salad, Thousand Island Dressing – maybe even a little wine. We had, would you believe, bologna, tomatoes and bread! I was to find out that this was to be the Saturday night meal for the next year and a half of my life. True, this was a Sunday, but this meal was considered a special treat.

It seemed strange that there were no speeches of welcome, no "Thank You" speeches to me and to the other seventy-four girls who had decided to dedicate their young lives to Religion. There were only more prayers and more bowing, and then we sat and ate in silence, except for the voice of one of the older postulants as she sat reading to us at a table on an elevated platform. She was reading from some holy book. I don't remember which book, but I do remember that it was not one that I had on my list of books.

The small bite of bologna sandwich stuck in my throat. I felt self-conscious. I hadn't met any of the newcomers, so I couldn't tell which were the old-timers and which were those who were sitting there scared to death like I was.

The postulant stopped reading – a small blessing because she was a lousy reader. She couldn't be heard anyway because it was time to wash the dishes. My sponsor's friend, The Postulant Mistress who I had been so smart with, sat at the front of the head table. She was built a little like King Henry VIII and now rang a small bell much like Henry must have done many times. This was a signal to some of the older postulants to bring large dishpans on trays to the table. The dishes were scraped in smaller pans and then washed and dried at the table. They were then placed in drawers in these same tables. I wondered what Emily Post would say about that. I hadn't had an occasion to add any of her books to my list, but I had a feeling she wouldn't have approved.

After dishes, prayers and more bowing, we walked through the basement halls, out the back door and over to the Novitiate – all in silence. I found out later that all postulants and novices were always to use the basement halls leading up to the chapel and not the main hall that we had used that first day. Postulants and novices were not to be seen in the main hall of the Motherhouse because the high potentates of The Order were afraid that we might do something stupid in front of an important guest who might be visiting.

The Novitiate consisted of two classrooms, a small chapel, a study hall for the novices and another for the postulants, and an office for the novice mistress. The novices' dorms were upstairs, and the sewing room, ironing room, bathroom and the novices' trunk room were in the basement. The basement walls were lined with pigeon-hole type boxes where we were to keep our textbooks, etc. I was to spend many hours of my next six months in this building.

We had evening recreation with the novices on that first evening. Recreation did not mean tennis, swimming or golf. It meant that we could talk! I was to find out later that recreation with the novices was a rare treat. Every day was spent in silence; it was considered a fault to talk to another postulant, but a greater fault to talk to a novice, or, heaven forbid, a professed sister. There was an hour's recreation period every evening, but usually only with other postulants. So, to spend an hour talking to a novice was considered by some to be the next best thing to being one.

A bell rang. Recreation was over. We filed back to the chapel, via the underground passageway, for night prayer.

Shortly after night prayer, another bell rang, the profound silence bell. It was a fault to break silence, and a really big fault to break profound silence. My guardian angel led me to the third floor of the Motherhouse and to my bed. The bed, with its accompanying stand and chair, was in a huge room, with about four aisles of beds, stands and chairs. There were curtains that could be pulled around the beds for privacy. I was in the biggest of the dorms. Some people were in a "semi-private" dorm, only ten people in those dorms, but because I was one of the youngest of the bunch, only seventeen, I didn't get such privileges.

I draped my postulant outfit on the chair and climbed into my long, white nun's nightgown. These gowns were huge. During the period when we were gathering my clothes together, mom had gotten a laugh when the nightgowns were delivered. She said,

"These gowns are big enough for two. I know that nuns are suppose to have a companion with them wherever they go, but this is ridiculous."

My mother sewed my aprons and skirts for me. Now that I think of it, this must have been very difficult for her considering that she didn't want her first born, or any of her children, for that matter, to leave her and join the convent, but here I was, my first night in The Nun Factory.

Chapter 2
More Fun and Games

Five A.M. The first bell of the day. Twenty minutes to get dressed and down to chapel for morning prayer, meditation and Mass. This sounded like a lot of time, but when you consider everyone who had to stand in line to use the facilities, wash your face, brush your teeth – it wasn't a lot of time.

On this first morning they did give us extra time. They even let us line up with a partner downstairs in the main hall before going into morning prayer. My partner and I started our first full day by breaking silence. We introduced ourselves and just had enough time to make a few remarks to make the other feel that they were not in this thing alone.

It seems that when people are starting out on a new adventure they tend to remember the first person that they meet long after the adventure is over. This gal, a brand new Sister, standing not more than five foot; round, ruddy face, eyes bright and sparkling, ready for this new adventure to begin, became my best friend for the next few years.

She started the adventure with me, but her postulancy lasted longer than mine. She had to have an emergency appendectomy after about three months into her postulancy. Sister Mary Postulant Mistress remained with her the entire time. While under the anesthetic it seems as though my friend said a few things about our Postulant Mistress that no Catholic girl, let alone a young girl aspiring to be a Catholic Sister, should have said.

After she recovered, my friend was told that she wouldn't be receiving the habit with the rests of us. Thus proving that everything she had said about the Postulant Mistress was indeed true.

But that was in the future, this was now. There were so many new things that first morning. First of all, as we made our way to our place in the chapel, we had to step around the novices and professed sisters who were prostrating themselves on the floor. They would kneel down, extend their scapular before them, then bend down and kiss their scapular. The scapular is a piece of cloth that goes over the head and extends down the front and the back. Later on we were told that this was done, morning and evening, as a symbol of submission to God. But, to us, on that first morning, stepping around all those nuns, in different stages of going down and coming up; it was more like an obstacle course.

Breakfast was also a new experience. For the next year and a half, we would have grapefruit or oranges and cereal. The cereal was the kind that came in little packages. With about ten of us per table, sometimes you got something good like Raisin Bran or Rice Krispies, then there were other mornings when you had just plain Corn Flakes.

But whatever the cereal, we usually ended up staring at it, sopping up milk. Everything would be going along fine until the reader made a mistake or somebody put an elbow on the table. The Postulant Mistress would ring that damn bell and the bran would hit the fan. Everything would stop while we gazed at a new creation called a cereal float and listened to her rant and rave at the offender.

Following the after breakfast prayers we would gather around this sweet lady while she quizzed us on the morning meditation. At 5:30 A.M. it wasn't always easy to stay awake. Many times I had no idea of what the meditation was about. Luckily, I avoided being called on even once at these morning game shows by maneuvering behind one of the refectory pillars until "Twenty Questions" was over.

Chapter 3
Letters, We Get Letters
We Get Stacks and Stacks
of Letters

After breakfast and a brief stop at the dorm to make our bed and get our books, we were off to our first college classes. There were some postulants who had already graduated from college. (We always said that they had given their old bones to the Community.)

But most of us were just starting. That summer all of us took the required English Composition I and II – among other courses. There was a set of identical twins in The Order, one taught English Composition I, the other II. They had similar names in religion as befitted twins. I wouldn't be surprised to find out that The Order had assigned these two to us green postulants to further confuse us. One of the more observant of the postulants came up with something that was of immeasurable help to us. Sister Mary English Composition II always carried an umbrella with her, so that solved that problem.

Often we would be able to pick up our mail before class. Many times I would stand at the end of the hall while I read my mother's letter and fight the homesickness that I felt before going into Sister Mary Umbrella's Comp II class.

Mom would keep me informed about all of the happenings at home plus all of the happenings on our soap operas. I knew all of the characters, so it wasn't necessary for her to say that these were soap opera characters. She'd just write, "Ray was sentenced for the murder of Marie, Joe raped Ellen, and Tony divorced Sue so that he could marry Judy, not knowing that Judy was his sister."

I appreciated knowing what was happening but you can imagine my panic when I found out that Sister Mary Postulant Mistress censored both our incoming and outgoing mail. I told mom that she had better stop her version of The Soap Opera Digest, because I was afraid my superior would think that all of these people committing incest, adultery, and being just down-right stupid, were my relatives. Even if they were doing all of these things while having amnesia, it still didn't excuse them.

As far as answering these letters, I got into the habit (no pun intended) of writing home a little at a time. Every night I'd sit in bed and write what had happened that day. The Postulant Mistress quickly put a stop to this, though. Sunday afternoon was the scheduled time for letter writing and she didn't want us to have our letters done ahead of time. This notion probably took root when she was a classroom teacher. Rule: Never let a kid work ahead, because then what are you going to do with him when he's done?

One Sunday afternoon we were seated at the long tables in the postulancy, obediently writing our letters, when one of the postulants leaned over, looked at my letter, thought it funny, grabbed it, stood up and began reading my description of, and the goings on in The Nun Factory. Part of me wanted her to stop because, after all, letters are supposed to be private. This one should have been seen only by my family, and, of course, the censor. The other part of me wanted her to go on because I kind of liked everyone thinking I was so clever and amusing. Just as I was wondering what to do, the Postulant Mistress came out of her office, saw what was going on, then promptly put an end to this exhibitionist.

My mother kept these letters. About fifteen years later she showed them to me. I asked if I could keep them. When I had privacy I read them, wept, and destroyed them. It was like looking at one's own baby picture. The person who wrote these letters, in a way, no longer existed.

Chapter 4
The College Degree of BS MS (more of the same) and PhD (piled higher and deeper)

In addition to the required college courses, like English Composition I and II, we had to take "Methods in Teaching" courses. I didn't think about my being a teacher until I was sitting in a class where the teacher was teaching prospective teachers how to teach. (I wonder if this teacher had a teacher who taught her how to teach prospective teachers how to teach.) When people back home had asked me if I had a boyfriend, I could look at them with disdain and say, "Of course not, I'm going to be a nun!" It never dawned on me that I was also going to have to teach.

All that I remember about that class was that it met in the late morning, right after Comp class. We met in the library which was right over the bakery section of the Motherhouse. This was very distracting because the smell of freshly baked bread at that hour was hard to take.

We had a "Methods in Teaching Reading" class every afternoon. The Sister who taught this course was a former reading consultant. She had been "recalled" because she was so autocratic and she was the same way in our "Methods" class. One day I wondered aloud how she could have been the only one in the whole diocese who knew how to teach reading. My blurting this out in class did not endear me to her.

She would tell us that if we taught a class for one hour, we should spend two hours in preparation for the class. With a seven-hour school day, plus all the hours of prayer, I suspected that she never took the "Methods in Math" class because her theory was mathematically impossible.

It seemed that if the class was held in the high school, the Motherhouse or the Novitiate, I would do well. But if the class was in one of the college buildings, I wouldn't.

The college nuns were unmerciful. Evidently they thought that we had unlimited time to spend preparing for their classes. We would have if we could have skipped going to prayer as they sometimes did.

The Catholic School System was doing a booming business back then and it was necessary to get in as many courses as possible during our postulancy and novitiate so that they could get warm bodies in front of all of those classrooms. When we received the veil of the professed sister it was believed, I guess, that we would also receive infused knowledge. This would make up for any lack in our education.

If it didn't, our transcripts would. When I saw my complete transcript years later, I was surprised to see that I had been given one semester hour in Liturgical Singing just for learning how to chant The Office of the Blessed Virgin, and two semester hours in Clothing for making my first habit. I would wear that habit at the end of the first six months.

One of the kids in my crowd was very interested in Science. She and I would go down to the Novitiate garden every afternoon and work on getting Biology and Zoology terms into my head. I squeaked through with a D in both subjects.

My sewing abilities were minimal. I had taken Clothing in high school. In fact, I took it for two years because I was so bad at it the first year. I was scared stiff of the nun who taught it. She wanted us to show our work to her at the end of every step. I would baste something on Monday and rip it out on Tuesday and start all over on Wednesday to avoid going up to her to show her my work. Luckily, the only sewing we had to do at the beginning of our postulancy was to sew a clean, white band to our black veil every week. This was "by hand". I would usually wait until late Saturday night, do a hurry-up job, stand up and find that I had sewn the veil to my bathrobe. This would be a great way to crack everyone up during profound silence.

The good news about my Nun Factory education was that I did get a college degree. I probably wouldn't have if I hadn't gone there. The bad news was that if left me with an eighteen semester hour deficiency when, years later, I tried to transfer my teaching license from one state to another. After earning a masters degree, I still found myself having to take undergraduate courses to qualify to teach in a different state.

Chapter 5
Stay Free Maxi Pads, 101 Uses

The Catholic faith has something called "adoration of the Blessed Sacrament". The host, believed by Catholics, to be the Body and Blood of Christ, is placed in a golden object called a monstrance and placed on the altar so that all can see.

The Motherhouse had special permission from Rome to have perpetual adoration. The Blessed Sacrament was "exposed" (always liked that term) soon after breakfast, and wasn't placed back into the tabernacle until after the afternoon prayers. The Blessed Sacrament was never to be left alone, so we were to choose a half-hour period when we weren't in class, for our adoration period.

One of the novices would usually lead the rosary during this time, with the rest of us answering the prayers. Postulants had a regular five-decade rosary, the novices and the professed sisters had the full fifteen decade rosary. As an added penance, most of us would say the rosary with arms outstretched. The postulants would take their rosaries off of their aprons, but the Novices would leave part of their rosary on their belt. Often this would lead to quite a tangle. It was mildly amusing to see everyone trying to keep their arms held in one position. One Sister's arms would be dropping just about the time another was regaining strength and bringing her arms back up. Try holding your arms outstretched for fifteen minutes if you don't get the picture.

This half-hour period was only a small portion of the time kneeling. Some enterprising nun thought about using some of the half-year supply of sanitary napkins that we had to bring from home to help alleviate our sore knees. All that you had to do was attach a napkin to each knee with a rubber band. Being basically chicken, I never tried this new invention. I had visions of them slipping off and falling right at the feet of the Mother General or some other high potentate. With the advent of tampons, strapping them onto postulants' sore knees is probably the only use that sanitary napkins have now.

Chapter 6
We Are Family
I've Got All My Sisters With Me

My hometown had very few vocations to the sisterhood. It was a Protestant town. But, more importantly, it was a town where one of the grade school nuns had run off with the parish priest. This occurred years before I had even started grade school, so it happened at a time when this was really frowned upon. Now, when you say, "Sister Mary Loose ran way with Father Fast, they're living in California where he is now a minister in the Episcopalian Church". The response from most would be a bored "Oh?"

But in those days it was a disgrace. People in our town were suspicious of the nuns from then on. My Sophomore English nun was the only one who ever gave us kids any indication of what it was like to be a nun in our city. She'd sit at her desk, lean her elbows on the desk, cup her hands around her mouth and say, "I want to get out of this burg".

After the elopement of the nun and the priest there was a long, dry spell when it came to religious vocations and some of those first vocations didn't last. I had to have a trunk for all of my things when I entered the convent. Where do prospective nuns buy a trunk? From ex-nuns! I bought my trunk from an ex-sister who left because she couldn't take wiping kids' noses anymore.

There was a certain high school in a big city that contributed five girls to The Nun Factory the year that I entered. This high school had the exact opposite reputation of my school and city. The Postulant Mistress loved this school and favored the girls who were from there. The girls were outgoing, bordering on brash and I never saw one of them hiding behind the refectory pillars. They were always alert and knew the answer. Surprisingly, I liked every one of them. They took the heat off of us shy, retiring types.

My dad had a theory about vocations. He was sure that the more girls sponsored by any given nun, the more commission that nun received. I don't know if dad ever thought about how this commission was paid. Nuns, in those days, never were given money. Maybe dad thought they were paid like the Indians – in beads – in this case, rosary beads.

One of these girls really had it made with The Postulant Mistress because, not only did she enter The Nun Factory, but so did her older sister, some two or three years before.

I have sisters who are twins. They were thirteen when I entered The Nun Factory. I wrote to them and tried to encourage them to join me. I thought I'd try anything to make life easier. But

I knew down deep that my attempt would be in vain. The twins had discovered boys soon after their First Communion and boys had no place in The Nun Factory.

Chapter 7
Audrey Hepburn,
You Ain't Seen Nothing Yet

The daily schedule was all important. There were no deviations. Five AM, wake-up bell, morning prayer, mediation, Mass, breakfast, morning classes, noon prayers, lunch, more classes, prayer, dinner, recreation, evening prayer.

But, on a beautiful, sunny fall Saturday afternoon, we were to report to the college auditorium because we were to get to see- what? – a movie? How worldly! The movie turned out to be – what else could it be, but – "The Nun Story" with Audrey Hepburn.

And, as luck would have it, I had a terrible cold. The kind where your nose is stuffed, your eyes water and you ache all over.

I had spent most of the morning trying to find The Postulant Mistress to ask permission to go back to bed. Yes, I was seventeen, but I was in The Nun Factory, so I had to ask permission to do anything out of the ordinary.

Finally, right before it was time to line up and walk to the movie, (yes, I was seventeen, but I couldn't walk to the auditorium on my own, I had to walk in line with the other postulants) I broke silence and asked one of the other postulants to tell The Postulant Mistress that I was sick and was going to bed.

I went upstairs to the big dorm. It was the first time that I had been alone in about three months. Everyone on campus was following the schedule, but I was out of the loop and it felt wonderful. I got into my huge, white gown, snuggled under the covers and was soon in a deep, probably slightly feverish sleep.

Soon the beautiful sleep was broken. Somehow I was now wide awake and aware that I was not alone. I turned over on my back and looked toward the foot of the bed. There was The Postulant Mistress in all of her glory, hovering over me. She looked larger that ever and her face was red because she was furious with me.

She said, "You are the type of person who always does exactly what she wants. Get up out of that bed. Get dressed and join the rest of the Sisters."

I was really hurt and puzzled because I didn't remember anytime when I had disobeyed. It was years later before I questioned anything that was done in those six months. Years later, too, much had been written about "tough love". These nuns had this concept down pat, long before it became popular.

Mom said that she always thought of me when she saw Audrey Hepburn in "The Nun Story". Years later I had the opportunity to see the movie in its entirety. The religious formation portrayed in that movie was very true to life. But, as for that first opportunity to see "The Nun Story", I'm sorry, but I don't remember much of it. I was too busy living it.

Chapter 8
Reunited and It Feels So Good

Children of the 40's were not left at day-care centers, probably because there weren't any day-care centers in the 1940's. My sisters and I weren't even left with a babysitter. The only summer camp that we were aware of was the one that Spin and Marty went to in a segment of "The Mickey Mouse Club".

My parents didn't go anywhere without us. Vacations were spent with them and with extended family members: aunts, uncles, cousins.

What's my point: My point is I was awfully homesick. But three months had passed and the nuns who ran the assembly line at The Nun Factory felt that we were indoctrinated to the point that we could stand to see our folks without losing our vocation. I wonder if they ever considered that our parents were instrumental in our having this calling to religious life in the first place. Needless to say, there were no "Suggestion Boxes" at the Motherhouse, so I couldn't mention this idea to them.

It must have been a Sunday in October, 1958. I have some pictures of the occasion – black and white – which was good because black and white were my colors for those six months. My parents, my sisters, my maternal grandparents, an aunt and uncle and their two children, made the five hour trip.

I look at the pictures, but I don't remember what we talked about. Everything was contained on the lawn. The Motherhouse didn't offer refreshments, let alone a meal to all of these travelers – families of all of the postulants. But there is a picture of me and I'm eating, (what's new?) so my family must have brought food. The only thing I remember about the day was something that my grandfather did.

My grandfather was probably about sixty at the time. He was born on December 27, two days after Christmas. One of his irreverent sons said that grandpa had a Messiah complex because his birthday was so close to Christ's birthday. But grandpa was very Christ-like. As far as I know, he never uttered an unkind word to or about anyone. He made every one of his many grandchildren feel that they were special.

He was reverent at Sunday Mass, and after Mass, he would go to the hospitals and visit the sick. Even his occupation was pretty close to Christ's; he owned an antique and upholstery business. You would walk into his shop and he always had upholstery tacks in his mouth and was busy hammering; upholstering furniture.

Anyway, grandpa was not in his coveralls this day. He was in dress pants, white shirt and tie. He was here to see his second oldest grandchild, his oldest granddaughter. I was only seventeen and he was my grandfather. I owed him respect. But, as I started to sit on one of the benches, on the lawn, that October Sunday, he said, "Wait." He took out his clean, white handkerchief, opened it and spread it out on the bench so that I could sit on it. I was only seventeen and he was my grandfather. But, in his eyes, I was a nun and deserved respect. Wow!

Chapter 9
On the Job Training

In addition to the college courses and hours of prayer, we were given what was called an "obedience". I don't know why it was called that, but on the outside world it would be defined as a job.

I was given two obediences or jobs. One was a very important and special job and that was to clean a bathroom over in one of the college buildings.

So, every day I would go from the Motherhouse, through the tunnel, to the college. I would then go to the little closet to get my bucket and supplies and clean the toilets, clean the sinks and mop the floor - all of the time working around the college girls who had to use the bathroom. The girls would look at this little figure in black and they would condescendingly smile. It could have been a good lesson in humility, but I hated it.

My second obedience was to spend an hour each day over in the laundry folding sheets. With around two thousand nuns on campus during the summer, you can imagine how many sheets were used. The system was to find a partner and start folding – "hot off the press". To pass the time and because we were nuns, we recited the rosary while we worked. We couldn't use our rosaries because we were folding sheets, but we would keep track by saying, "One, Hail Mary" and then proceed with the rest of the prayer, "Two, Hail Mary" etc. There are supposed to be ten "Hail Mary's" to a decade. I have a feeling that sometimes the Blessed Mother got ten, sometimes nine, sometimes eleven, and if it was really hot in the laundry, maybe as few as seven. But our hearts were in the right place.

All of these obediences kept a young nun off of the streets and out of the pool halls.

Chapter 10
May I Show You To a Table?

Every day we were to find some time when The Postulant Mistress was in her office. Her office was really just a little alcove in the postulants' workroom.

She would be sitting at her desk. We would come in, one by one, kneel down beside her and confess our faults. A "fault" could be anything from breaking silence to breaking things. Sometimes I would try confessing "breaking silence and things", all in one breath, hoping that The Postulant Mistress wouldn't notice the "things" part of it. If we broke something she'd always want to know what it was, and that could sometimes get you into deeper trouble.

You had to tell how many times you had committed the fault. If it was breaking silence, you had to say if it was profound silence or just plain regular silence. She also wanted to know whom you had talked to.

There was also something called "custody of the eyes". You were to keep your eyes cast down at all times - not gawking around and looking at everything. It was a fault to not keep custody of the eyes.

I don't remember what kind of penance we had to do for the minor faults, probably say additional prayers. I do remember what the penance was for bigger faults – it was a floor dish.

If you were given a floor dish as a penance, it meant that you had to eat your meal while sitting on the refectory floor. The smart thing was to find a pillar to prop up your back and you sat with legs out straight. It really wasn't so bad.

Who ever had the job of serving that day brought you your meal. You even had your own salt and pepper!

Floor space was limited, so there was always a waiting list of people waiting to "take their floor dish". I think, to this day, I still owe them seventeen or eighteen floor dishes.

Chapter 11
You See Them Come, But
You Don't See Them Go

We started out seventy-five strong. Seventy-five young women filled with religious zeal. But, little by little, the zeal was overcome by homesickness, or being beaten down, or maybe a combination of the two.

Twenty-five girls left between June 28 and December 31-six months. And I never ever saw one of them go. Everyone asks, "Did they shave your head?" No, they didn't shave our heads, but our hair was cut pretty short. So, being a born detective, I did wonder when I would see a young sister, at night, in the dormitory, with hair that was getting a little long. And I really wondered when that same nun had curlers in her hair. Why, in the world, would a nun be wearing curlers? Where was she going and who was she going to see? And why would you curl your hair, only to put a veil over it?

The real suspicion came when she wasn't at breakfast the next morning. I don't know how they got them out of there without our seeing them. I don't know if their parents came to get them. I don't know if they were put on a bus. I don't know how many were asked to leave. I would be willing to bet that almost one hundred percent of them wanted to get out of there, because I gave them reason to ask me to leave and they didn't. Who would mop the floors, clean the toilets and fold the sheets? They certainly wouldn't hire someone to do that when they had me!

So, as we neared the end of our six months, saw our postulancy coming to a close and looked forward to receiving the habit, we also saw a lot of empty places at the breakfast table.

Chapter 12
The Plant Died, Better It Than Me

The Advent Season, the time of spiritual preparation before the coming of the Baby Jesus on Christmas Day, was doubly important to us this year because this was our first Christmas in The Nun Factory.

The Postulant Mistress told us of the retreat that we would be on before receiving the habit. I couldn't imagine how we could "retreat" any more. We had left our parents and families, we were silent most of the day, we worked, studied and prayed all of the day. We had seen our family only once in six months. There, of course, were no phone calls allowed. But here, in the midst of this deep retreat, comes a phone call – for me! The Novice Mistress, who had never spoken to me in her entire life, gave me the message. Seems like the call was from one of my uncles. The Novice Mistress told me that she'd let me take the call because it might have to do with traveling plans. Our families were allowed to come and see the ritual of our receiving the habit. She also informed me that taking this phone call was very much against the spirit of the retreat and to make it quick.

I got on the phone and my uncle told me that he had bought a plant as a gift to give me on this special occasion, but said, "Lo, and behold, the plant died!" He told me that he saw this as a sign that I should not go through with this. I told him "thank you" but that I was going through with it.

We were dressed in bridal gowns and veils, for we were becoming brides of Christ. The chapel was filled with our families. After the first part of the ceremony, we left and then came back in the chapel in full habit. Only the veil was different, it was white instead of black, because we were novices now, we were not yet professed sisters.

Following the ceremony, my dad came looking for me. Mom was very upset. I'm sure that she thought that at some point I would leave and come home. But here was one more hurdle that I had passed.

There was one more year in The Nun Factory before we would go "out on mission", which meant that we would go out into the world, still live with other nuns in a convent, but we would start to teach.

This is how I spent the late 1950's, all of the 60's and the early 70's – a total of thirteen years. Mom never did get her wish. I never did come home to live. I was thirty by the time that I left the convent. It was way past time to let my hair grow, put it up in curlers and make my getaway.

June 28, 1958. This was the day that I entered the convent, the day that I said "good-bye" to my family and began my time in The Nun Factory. The smile says, "You have no idea what you're getting into."

December, 1958. This was my first day "in the habit". I had finished my six months as a postulant and was beginning the year of being a novice.

December 1958. This, again, is my first day wearing the habit. And, again, as the smile shows, I was still clueless.

And Other Horror Stories
#1

When I told people that I was working on a book, they would ask, "What's the title?" When I would say, "The Nun Factory and Other Horror Stories" they would laugh. I've told you about "The Nun Factory", now it's time to tell you some "Other Horror Stories". I'm sure, by now, that you don't expect any real "horror stories". What follows is just a few other funny things that I heard about when I was in the convent.

Before you can understand the first story, I must explain one of the Catholic beliefs. It's called the "Immaculate Conception". This is the belief that Mary, because she was going to be the mother of Christ, was free from original sin. Many Catholics believe that Mary appeared to a girl named Bernadette at Lourdes in 1958. When Bernadette asked who she was, Mary replied, "I am the Immaculate Conception".

Ok, here's the story. After the first year of teaching we were preparing to go back to The Nun Factory for the summer and continue our college work. As an "end of the year gift" one of the superiors gave a study light to all of her young nuns. This light clamped onto your head and you could study after "lights out". The light looked like it was shining out of your forehead. Needless to say it was not allowed. There was an old nun at The Nun Factory that would go around and check to see if all lights were out for the night and make you go to bed if you weren't already there.

One of the recipients of this light had been in my class. In fact, she was the one who had an older sister that had also entered The Nun Factory. Her superior warned all of the Sisters not to get caught with this light. She especially warned this Sister. She said, "I'm worried about you. What will you say if the old nun catches you with that light?"

The young sister said, "I will slowly rise. She will see me in my long, white nightgown. That light will be coming from my forehead and I will say 'I am the Immaculate Conception!'"

Horror Story
#2

As I mentioned before, one of the Catholic beliefs is that Christ is present in the host and this is called the Blessed Sacrament. To show that the Blessed Sacrament is present in a church or chapel, the sanctuary lamp is lit. A sanctuary lamp is a candle within a red glass.

Well, it seems that one evening a nun was doing some Spring cleaning in the convent chapel. She moved the sanctuary lamp out of the chapel and near the convent's front door so that she could do some mopping.

Soon after, the doorbell rang. She went to the door and standing in front of her was a handsome, well-dressed gentleman. When he saw this nun, in full habit, his jaw dropped and he quickly backed away from the front door, brightly lit by the red sanctuary lamp.

As I said before, the superiors at The Nun Factory should not have been called Postulant Mistress and Novice Mistress.

They should have been called Madams.

Horror Story
#3

When this particular Nun Factory was built, there was nothing surrounding it but farm land. So the Mother General, the supreme head of this young Order, allowed the Sisters to keep some chickens and cows.

It was now some fifty years later and the Mother General was on her death bed. She was surrounded by the high potentates of The Order. These Sisters had been led by her for many years. The prayers of over 2,000 other Sisters of her Order were with her.

The Sisters in her room were listening intently for any words of wisdom that would come from her lips, but she seemed to only mutter about things from the past.

Suddenly she became very agitated. One of the nuns suggested that she fix some warm milk for their beloved Mother. Everyone present agreed that this was a good idea.

Sister warmed the milk and then, as an after thought, added some brandy, with the hope that this would also help in calming her down.

Mother General sipped the milk and the Sisters noticed a little color coming to her cheeks. She sipped some more and feebly raised herself on one elbow. She looked as if she was about to speak and the Sisters leaned closer to hear what was to be her last words. She slowly looked at every one of them and said, "Sisters, don't ever get rid of that cow!" Words to live by.

About the Author

Joining the convent enabled Barb to go to college and earn a Bachelor's and Master's Degree. It also gave her the opportunity for a career in education, but she's also dabbled in sales (cemetery property, of all things) and has also been a co-owner of a restaurant (even though she doesn't cook).

During all of these busy years, she's wanted to tell of her experience in joining a religious order. She tells her story with much humor and just a tad of irreverence.

So, we will find the answers to some deep, spiritual questions, such as: " Did nuns really shave their heads?" and "What other uses did nuns have for stay-free Maxi pads?"

A fun story and a fast read.

Made in the USA
Monee, IL
29 December 2022

23949077R00049